For my loving husband Irv,

without whom this book

could never have been written.

Designing from the Stone

Design Techniques for Metal Clay

Using the Stone as Inspiration

By

Lisa Barth

Acknowledgements:

Editing: Kim Chambers, Francesca Watson

If you have any questions or comments about this book, please contact: www.lbjewelrydesigns.com

Table of Contents

We have met the enemy and he is us.
-- Pogo

Thoughts on Art and Fear

I have a confession to make; I am a rock-aholic. I love stones, their colors, textures, fascinating patterns, and sparkle. Don't even get me started on drusy; my heart races! Ever since I was knee high to a grass-hopper I have loved stones. Finding my first geode on the banks of the Mississippi river, the mystery and beauty of that sparkling crystal captured my heart. Even now as an adult I can't go anywhere where there is dirt and resist the temptation of looking through it to see what treasures it may hold. My ever growing stash of stones always has room for a few more. Couple this love of stones with a steely determination to learn and *Designing from the Stone* was born. But I wasn't always like this; the words steely and determined would never have been used to describe me just a few years ago.

For years I saw myself as unexceptional, so terribly average and lost in the sea of mediocrity. Being rather timid by nature didn't help me and I was too afraid of failure to take the risk of trying something new. Why bother? There was always too much pain involved when I found out after putting all that effort in, I did not measure up anyway. My greatest fear would be realized: I just wasn't good enough.

But what does this phrase "good enough" mean? What was I doing that wasn't good enough and who was it that I wasn't good enough for? In the Art world I would hear the word talent used quite often. This special, inborn ability to create beauty seemed to be bestowed upon only the lucky few. Every time I tried something new and it would turn out so wonderfully mediocre, it confirmed the fact that I certainly wasn't one of the chosen few. And what is worse, I had equated great work with attaining a level of perfection that was completely unrealistic, consequently setting myself up for failure before I even began. But despite this internal battle, my urge to create was too strong and I muddled onward in my creative journey.

Creating Art is chancy; uncertainty of the outcome is certain to happen. Learning how to embrace this, even welcoming the fact that we cannot control everything, brings with it the possibilities of the unknown. There is discovery in the journey of creating. Taking risks, stepping out, daring to say to yourself that you have something of value in your point of view, no matter who or what comes against you gives greater meaning to the outcome and makes the finish that much sweeter. Lessons learned along the way are invaluable. I always learn more when things go wrong than when things goes smoothly. It only means I have to dig deeper and try a bit harder and inevitably the mountainous problem has turned to a manageable molehill. But more importantly, I have learned.

It is my most heartfelt wish that you too can find great joy in your journey as you embrace and learn the uncertainty of the creative process. You *are* good enough, *more than* good enough and there is great value in what you will attain if you push yourself, reach for it and let go of your fear.

Basic Metal Clay Tools

Work surface

Wire cutters

Needle files of various sizes and shapes

Olive oil or release agent of your choice

Texture mats (optional)

Deck of Cards

Clay roller

Needle tool

Silicone tipped clay shaper

Small, round #1 brush

Flat #4 brush

Water in a cup

Plastic wrap

Tissue blade

Sandpaper or sanding pads – 600, 400, 320 grits

Brass brush

Liquid dish soap

Rubber block

Agate burnisher

Tweezers (preferably cross-lock with heat-resistant fiber grip)

Round nose pliers

Flat nose pliers

Materials for Bezel Setting

Stone cabochon

Fine silver tabbed bezel wire

25 grams of Art Clay Silver 650

Art Clay Syringe type

Art Clay Paste type

White paper

Lisa's Favorite Tools

Of all the tools I use, these tools I find are very helpful in creating concise, refined pieces. They are not expensive, they just work and I find them invaluable in cutting and refining metal clay.

Ultra Clay Pick: This super fine needle tool cuts metal clay like butter. Fantastic! Find it at www.CoolTools.com.

Make up applicators: These little sponges on a stick are wonderful for smoothing out surfaces on larger areas. Get them wet and rub the surface of the clay lightly until the water loosens the surface. Use them to literally redistribute the top surface of metal particles in the clay. You can thank Pam East for this wonderful tip. Thank you Pam!

Variety Pack Sanding Swabs: These little gems are wonderful for sanding rounded areas that are hard to get to. The pack contains 9 different grits and are 2.25 inch long swabs. Especially helpful with smoothing out hand carved areas and syringe patterns, the varying grits give you the ability to choose how coarse you want to sand. Find them at www.ArtClayWorld.com.

Clean Up Sticks: These tiny sanders reach into places that are hard to get to for cleaning up and smoothing out any rough areas. They are two sided, 280 grit on one side and 400 grit on the other. They are 1/8 of an inch wide and I find they fit into most tiny areas and make refining such a pleasure. Anything like that is just great to have around. I am crazy about them. Find them at www.naturescapesstudio.com

Jeweler's file: This file is made of Swiss steel so it is very strong even though it is so small. It has a rounded side and a flat side with a tapered tip. For refining the tiniest details, this file is the one I grab most often. The shape of the tool offers a variety of uses, according to what is needed for the design. Find them at www.jffjewelersupply.com.

Design: What's the Big Deal?   Part I

Design is the road map, the path by which you begin the journey of creating your art work. It is the choices you make that reveal your unique viewpoint. All art, be it visual art or architecture, music or mathematics share common elements of design. Design helps you solve problems, arrange and emphasize these elements. When they all come together intentionally, purposefully, they create a beautiful harmony in your work.

Design is what draws the eye of your viewer and keeps him interested and engaged. Successfully combining the elements of design with some good, basic principles of design can result in a harmonious piece that is a pleasure to see and will captivate your audience. So let's take a look and see what these elements are and how to go about applying them to your work.

Elements of Design

Each of these components is the physical characteristics that compose a piece of art.

Color

Color is the most expressive element of design. People will generally notice color first. Consequently, I believe it is very important to learn as much as you can about this highly expressive element. I will spend more time introducing color than any other element.

Color comes from the spectrum of light (distribution of light energy versus wavelength) interacting in the eye. Our modern understanding of light and color begins with Isaac Newton (1642-1726) and a series of experiments that he published in 1672. He was the first to understand the rainbow — he refracted white light with a prism, revealing its component colors: red, orange, yellow, green, blue and violet.

Properties of Color

Hue – the name of the color, such as blue or red

Value – the light or darkness of the hue

Intensity – the purity or saturation of the color

Temperature – the warmth or coolness of the color. Examples of this would be red being a warm color and blue being a cool color.

Although we cannot perceive the actual temperature of a color, people have color associations which lend certain qualities to the color perception.

Color Associations

Many people have clear associations with color. These associations can be very useful when designing with your stone. They may give you ideas from which you can develop the direction of the composition. Here are a few color associations people tend to have:

Red: love, passion, power, excitement, danger. He was "seeing red" he was so angry.

Yellow: happiness, wisdom, imagination with a strong negative side of cowardice. "He's yellow" meaning he has no guts.

Blue: serenity, sadness, innocence. He is in a "blue mood" or singing the "blues" expresses sadness.

Green: fertility, harmony and balance, peace, growth, calm with the negative side of "green with envy"

Violet: royalty, dignity, spirituality

Orange: ego, pride, flamboyance

Black: mystery, austerity, harshness, emptiness, death

White: purity, virtue, hope, innocence, youth, freshness

Pink: gentle qualities of red; maternal love and affection

The associations you make with the color of your stone can be very helpful to you while designing your piece. They can spark an idea and guide the inspiration to become the theme. In the piece to the right the vivid green of this Labradorite cabochon was associated with leaves and buds and was the inspiration to create this pendant. The intent was to represent the life contained in a bud, just waiting to unfold.

Color Theory

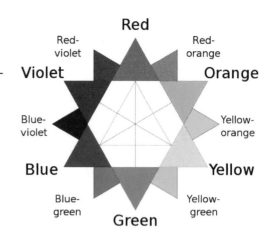

In the visual arts, color theory is guidance to color mixing and the visual impact of specific color combinations.

Color theory was originally formulated in terms of three primary colors—red, yellow and blue. It is from these three colors all other colors are derived from when mixed.

Complimentary Colors

These colors are located opposite of each other on the color wheel. When complimentary colors are placed next to each other, they will bring high contrast and intensity to each other. If you look at the color wheel you will see that red and green are located directly opposite each other. Consequently, placing two stones of complimentary colors next to each other will add energy to and enliven a composition.

In the picture to the left, the orange color of this Tigereye was given a little zing by placing a small, blue Lapiz cabochon next to it. Blue was chosen because it is the compliment of orange.

Analogous Colors

These colors are next to each other on the color wheel, such as blue and green. These colors are soothing together and tend to tone down a composition.

In the picture to the right a small blue sapphire was placed above the Chrysocolla cabochon. This blue color is calming and added a touch of sparkle to the composition. It also helped focus the attention at the top of the stone.

Monochromatic Colors

This is when only one color is used and the value of this color changes in the composition.

Line

Line is essentially a path between two points. It is a very powerful element. When used well, lines can lead the viewer's eye through the composition, giving points of interest and enhance the stone. A line can also be formed when two shapes meet. Lines can be implied if not complete. Your mind tends to connect the dots to form lines when they are placed on a geometrical pattern as people tend to seek out familiar or recognizable shapes.

Lines may imply motion, suggest direction, impose style and reveal emotion.

Types of Lines

Horizontal lines – imply calm or being at rest

Vertical lines – imply power or strength, stability

Diagonal lines – imply movement, action, change

Curved lines– imply quiet, sensual feelings

Spiral lines– imply curiosity, draw your eye in as a powerful attention getter

Radial lines – imply warmth, radiating heat, power

In the picture above, the radial lines in the design draw your attention to the center stone and imply radiating warmth. Lines placed in this way are a very powerful element help capture the attention of the viewer.

The radial lines were continued to the back side of the design.

7

Shape

Shape is essentially enclosed lines, the outline of an object. The positive shape is the area that is occupied by the subject and forms an outline. These shapes can be realistic, abstract or anything in between. Negative space is everything that is not your subject. The negative space is defined by the edges of the positive space and the edge of the back plate. Be mindful of the shapes you are creating within your composition as one element relates to another. Plan the structure of these shapes, both positive and negative to be interesting and to balance each other.

Shapes can be symbolic in many cultures. These common associations can be used in your composition to your advantage, to emphasize your design concept.

Circle – can symbolize unity, infinity

Triangle – can symbolize connectedness, home, trinity

Square – can symbolize a solid foundation, stability, reality

Rectangle – can symbolize grounding, solidarity, foundation

Spiral – can symbolize growth, cosmic motion, spirit

Texture

Texture is the surface quality or the feel of an object. It may be felt, like the rough edges of a brick or the softness of a silk scarf. For us metal clay artists, texture can be created by using various tools to impress into the clay or carve out portions of clay. The various depth of shadow created from the recessed or carved out areas can be used for strong visual impact or soft, subtle detail in the composition of the piece according to the artist's intent.

In the piece to the right the pattern from the Turquoise was mimicked in the design using syringe metal clay to give a deep texture.

Form

Form is the three dimensional aspect of an object. Shape is two dimensional, but form takes on the third dimension to give depth. In drawing or painting, shading a circle would make it into a sphere, giving it the appearance of height, width and depth.

As metal clay artists we can add form by sculpting, molding and forming this wonderful medium to create virtually any form we choose.

Value

Value is the light or darkness of an element. This can be used to show volume, depth or perspective within the composition.

Space

Space refers to the two di-mensional area on which you are composing your piece. Space is also referred to as a resting place for the eye. This area with little or no detail can balance and emphasize a textured or detailed area of your piece.

In the Sunset Jasper piece to the right, the border creating the frame around the stone and the smooth area surrounding the trees is referred to as an area of rest or space.

9

Principles of Design   Chapter 2

Principles of design describe the relationships between the elements of design, how they all work together in the composition. They are tools to be used in establishing focus, expressing a point of view or evoking emotion. Keeping these principles in mind while designing helps you make good decisions for creating a purposeful work, with an overall harmony of composition.

Balance

Balance is the placement of elements to establish equal visual weight on both sides of a composition. Good balance gives a sense of stability. Symmetrical balance is when there are identical elements on both sides. Asymmetrical balance is achieved when there are a variety of elements adding up to equal visual weight on both sides.

Visual weight refers to how strong an element is or how much impact it has in a composition. This can be due to many characteristics of the elements. If, for example, we are considering line, all things being equal, darker lines have more visual weight than lighter lines and thick lines have more than thin lines. They are noticed more and have more impact in the composition. In regards to shape, larger, darker or more intensely colored shapes will be noticed more than smaller, lighter ones. Texture also has visual weight. You can see this by observing how an area of texture demands your attention and holds it there, whereas an area that is sparsely textured does not. Densely textured areas draw the eye more and therefore demands attention be given to that area.

Emphasis

When designing a composition you have the ability to draw the eye from place to place or to simply emphasize an element within the stone. Most often this means creating a focal point, where the eye goes first. It plays the leading role, so to speak, and is the most predominant element. It is from there the viewer takes in the rest of the composition. All other elements should take on the supporting roles to emphasize the lead.

Repetition

Portions of the design can be introduced and repeated to provide unity and direction in the composition. Repetition can provide points of visual interest that can move the viewer's eye toward your focal area. It can also connect two elements together visually.

The tendency is to assume repetition means identical elements in regular or symmetrical intervals. This can be boring and predictable. Make an effort to throw in a bit of variation to liven up the pattern. In the picture to the right, the element of the spiral line in the shell was repeated in the bail. To give it slight variation, the direction of the spiral in the bail was reversed.

Finding a repeatable element within your stone doesn't mean that you have to repeat the entire pattern. It is often most effective to take part of what you see in the stone and mimic the feeling that pattern creates. In the picture to the left, the angles of double lines play off of the angles presented in this Chrysocolla cabochon. The lines take their cues from the stone but do not directly copy what is there. The lines mimic and support the chaotic nature of the stone and the general feeling it brings.

Contrast

Contrast is the use of opposing or dissimilar elements in a design. It is a strong tool to use to create visual impact and emphasis. It can also add excitement, attract attention or add dynamic flow throughout your composition. Contrast between opposite elements (such as big versus small, thick and thin, smooth and rough, organic and structured) makes your piece more interesting and enjoyable.

In the picture to the right, the smooth surface of the turquoise cabochon needed some contrasting texture to bring visual interest to the composition of the piece. The swirl pattern of the texture was chosen because it is in direct opposition to the geometric lines of the cabochon. A dark patina was added to bring some depth of color to the texture which also emphasizes the bright blue of the turquoise.

Movement

Movement is the flow of the line or the path that your eye will take as the elements direct which way to go. There are three basic types of movement in artwork, horizontal, vertical and diagonal. Horizontal movement, as discussed previously in the line segment, implies calm and serenity, vertical movement implies stability, power or strength and diagonal movement implies dynamic action.

In the picture to the left, the movement is diagonal, pulling your eye from the bail, through the stone and back down to the spot where the lines converge at the bottom of the pendant.

Rhythm

Rhythm comprises repeated forms, lines, colors or textures to create pattern or sequence. They should enhance the focal area and contribute to the movement of the composition.

In the picture to the right the rhythm was established by repeating the dynamic lines found in the Ammonite fossil in an orderly sequence to add to the motion of the spiral in the fossil. The circular motion and the direction of the lines all emphasize what is going on in the stone and help pull your eye around the composition.

Unity

Unity is the intentional choice and use of individual elements so that they interact and work together to achieve the artist's goal. They are stronger together than if they were on their own.

The elements chosen to work with this Lizard Skin Ammolite were radial lines playing off the angles of the stone and the repetition of the texture found within the stone. The lines converge at two points on either side of the stone. The intent was to draw the eye through the stone, creating an imagined horizontal line that connects the two points and balances the vertical orientation of the pendant.

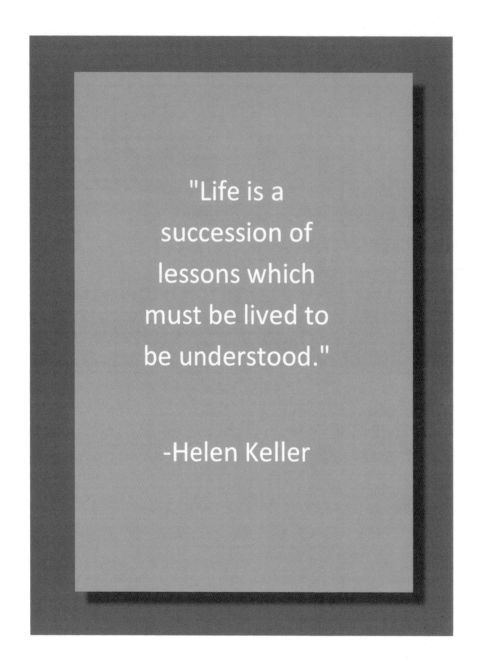

"Life is a
succession of
lessons which
must be lived to
be understood."

-Helen Keller

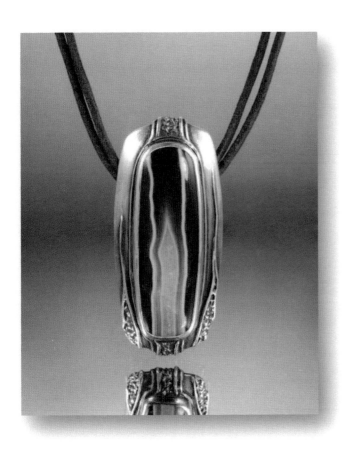

Part 2

The Process of Creating

Design is a tricky thing. At one moment it can be very illusive and seem to run from you, causing a great deal of stress in the creative process. Other times it flows freely from your mind into your hands, causing great joy in the journey. Let's take a look at this creative process of designing from the stone and see what it entails from beginning to end, from the analysis of the stone and conception of the design to the fabrication and finishing of the piece.

Start with a Great Stone

Your choice of stone is of critical importance with this method of design. You need to have some kind of connection with the stone; something about it has to inspire you. It can be as simple as a great color that you respond to. It can have wonderful texture or an amazing shape; whatever it is it needs to speak to you in some way so that you can use this as inspiration from which you derive direction to create a setting that sings a beautiful harmony between metal and stone.

Analyzing Your Stone   Chapter 3

Now that you've taken the time to understand a bit about how the elements and the principles of design work together, let's take a good look at how we go about applying this when designing a setting for a bezel- set stone. We start at square one with your stone. In this process, the stone is the most important element; therefore you begin by "listening" to what your stone has to say. Here is a worksheet that I find helpful in organizing my thoughts when I analyze my stone.

In two columns analyze what your stone has to offer (the Yes column) or what it does not have (the No column) in terms of three main elements, shape, texture and color. Write down what you see.

Yes	No
Shape --	Shape--
Texture --	Texture--
Color--	Color—

What to look for:

Shape—is the shape interesting by itself? Is the cut symmetrical or will it need additional elements to give it visual balance? Does the shape remind you of anything? If so, write these things down.

Texture—is there an abundance of texture within your stone? Do you see any patterns presented in the stone you'd like to repeat? Is there an area within the texture that intrigues you? Write down what you see and what you don't see; they are both important. What is not there is what you may want to add to the design.

Color—this element tends to give clues to the mood or style that suits the stone. Is the color bright or dull, exuberant or calm, highly visible or more subtle? If you follow these clues it can help you find the right style in which to design your setting. Does the color remind you of anything? Write it all down, it will help you make design decisions.

What to do with the Yes's and the No's

Prioritize what you like best.

In designing from the stone, the stone always has the leading role. Everything you decide to do should emphasize this lead.   To do this it is easiest to prioritize the things you like best about your stone.   What is it that intrigued you enough to purchase the stone in the first place? Most of the time, you will find these things have been written in the Yes column.   Keep them in mind when you start the designing process.

For this banded agate on page 15, the vertical lines that seemed to form a "candle " in the middle of the stone were chosen to be the main focal feature.

Here are my thoughts as I analyzed this stone before beginning to create the setting.

Yes	No
Shape-- I like the shape, I don't necessarily want	
to add anything to change the silhouette	
Texture--Love the vertical lines and the "candle"	
in the middle	
Color-- a little on the dull side but graphic enough	
to carry its own weight in the design	

There weren't any No's for this stone; however, the graphic simplicity of the lines within the stone and the delicate nature of the texture told me to keep the design simple and linear with just a touch of texture. This stone could be overwhelmed with a complex design and my goal is to enhance what the stone has to offer, not to overpower it.

Choose your supporting features.

Establish and clarify the features you'd like to add to the composition. In the No column, the things that you wrote down give you a clue as to what you can add to the composition to emphasize your leading role. What does your stone lack and therefore need to become a more dynamic piece? For example, does it have enough texture to be engaging? Is the color wonderful on its own or does it need a contrasting accent to spice things up a bit? For our example stone, the supporting features were the vertical lines inside the agate. The lines in the stone will be used as a design feature in the setting.

Decide what to do with the bail.

When designing a piece it can be effective to incorporate the bail into the design and make it an integral part of what is going on. After all, the bail has a major function; it holds your entire piece up so the world can see it. This is an important feature so don't overlook the power of the bail.

When choosing the bail design for the banded agate, I chose not to use an integrated bail on the front because it would interfere with the vertical lines that were to be the main supporting feature of the design. The bail would be place so that it would be integrated into the back design, hidden from view.

Integrated Bail

Here are some examples of designs that feature the bail as an integrated part of the design and also as a hidden bail on the back of a pendant.

In the piece to the left, the shape of the stone, with its flat top just screamed to have a big, bold bail. The color of the stone was strong enough to carry a bold design with heavy texture. The placement of a touch of the same textural element on the bottom of the pendant lends a vertical emphasis to the horizontal stone, giving some visual balance to the composition.

The bail in the Chrysocolla piece to the right was integrated into the design. It was intended to continue the flow of the line within the stone, like water cascading down a waterfall, through the stone and out at the bottom right corner of the pendant.

Hidden Bail

Conversely, if your stone doesn't lend itself well to a design with a big, obvious or integrated bail, you always have the option of placing the bail on the back, essentially hiding it from sight. This takes it out of the composition on the front but puts it directly in the back composition, giving a nice opportunity to embellish the back. In the Labradorite piece above, the bail was made with one long extruded piece of metal clay that looped around from the front to the back. The opportunity was taken to have some fun on the backside. Some details and flourishes that go along with the front were added so that the back can be seen as a continuation of the front.

Refine Your Ideas About Color

Determine how the color and texture of the stone influences the design. How does the color influence your thoughts? Does it make you think of something tangible that you could use in the design?

In this Picture Jasper pendant, the landscape in the stone presented lines that were extended in the metal clay to represent the mountain scene. The texture along the top portion was added to mimic stars in the night sky.

Refine your Ideas about Texture

As you consider what your stone offers in the way of texture, think through the possibilities that this design element provides and choose those which would bring out the unique beauty of your cabochon. In the piece above, the circular pattern and texture seen within the Ocean Jasper was repeated. The shape of the texture can change the shape of your back plate. As you study your stone and make choices in the design process, sometimes the texture by itself can influence the silhouette of the piece.

Texture does not have to be complicated; it can be very simple and still be quite effective. In the picture to the right, the fossil star fish was enhanced by simply extending the dots found in the stone onto the metal. The boldness of the star was enough and didn't require much to add to the setting.

Be intentional with your placement of your chosen elements and texture, be they bold or subtle. Every part is a piece of the whole that has to make sense as it fits together.

Making a Sketch

The next step in the creative process is to make a sketch of your design idea. Please don't overlook the importance of doing this. Making a sketch really helps you define what your thoughts are and gives you visual evidence whether they work with or against your stone.

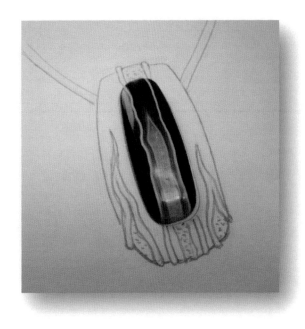

Step 1: Trace the shape of your stone on a blank piece of paper. Now draw a simple outline of what shape you want the back plate to be. This will establish the silhouette for your piece. In this case, I did not want to change the shape of the silhouette of the stone because I liked the shape. So I simply drew a bigger rectangle around the stone.

Step 2: Texture and lines are drawn in next. Within this stone I saw a candle and strong, vertical lines. With this in mind, lines were drawn that matched this pattern at the bottom and continued at the top, as if the lines were going through the stone. Then shapes were drawn to represent flames on either side of the cab. The texture repeated a pattern within the white part of the agate. A segment of this texture and line was placed at the top of the pendant to draw your eye upward through the piece.

Making Templates from Your Sketch

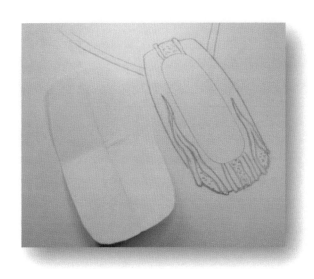

Take another sheet of paper and place it on top of the sketch that you have just made and trace the outline of the shape that will be the back plate. Cut out that shape. We will use this as a template for cutting out the metal clay when the time comes. Here in the picture you can see I have cut out the back plate template. The paper was folded twice and then cut out to make it easier to get a symmetrical shape.

Creating the Wire Bezel

Step 1: Wrap the bezel wire loosely around your stone with the tabbed edge toward the back of the stone. Shape the bezel wire so that it conforms to the shape of the stone but fits loosely. The stone should not have much "wriggle room" but it should fall out easily when you turn over the tabbed bezel wire. Give yourself a bit of extra length and cut long if you are unsure. It is better to have a bit too much and trim to fit than not enough.

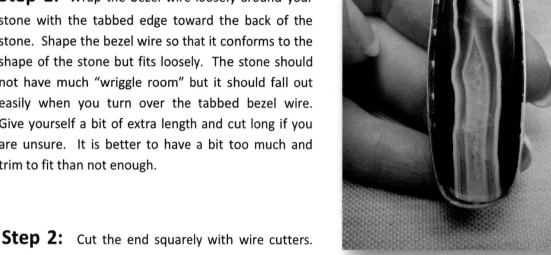

Step 2: Cut the end squarely with wire cutters. Mold and press the ends so they are flush against each other without any gaps.

The ends were placed at the eight o'clock position with this piece. There is no hard and fast rule to this. Place the seam where you think it will be the least conspicuous within your design. Try to avoid the 12 o'clock or the 6 o'clock position as these places usually receive a lot more visual attention than other areas around your stone.

Step 3: Place a few dots of Art Clay oil paste on the seam of the bezel wire and let it dry completely, 30 minutes at 210F/100C or for 24 hours at room temperature.

Fire the bezel wire at the standard firing schedule for Art Clay oil paste: ramp the kiln at full speed to 1472oF/800oC and hold for 30 minutes. Allow to air cool or quench in cold water.

Creating the Back Plate

Step 1: Roll out about 25 grams of silver metal clay to a thickness of 5 cards. Place your back plate template on top and cut out this shape using a needle tool. Put away all the surrounding metal clay in an air tight container.

Step 2: Place the bezel wire in the center of the wet metal clay and press down until the horizontal tabs are touching the surface of the metal clay. Don't press any farther than this or it will cause weak areas in the design where the metal clay isn't thick enough to withstand the pressure of shrinkage during firing.

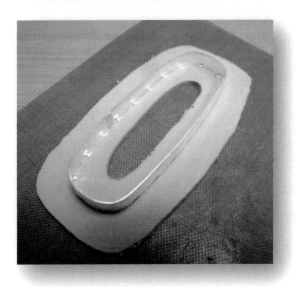

Many people ask me about what happens if you press in too far with the bezel wire. Well, here is a piece that has taken this tragic route. The tabs of the bezel wire pushed through to the back and caused tearing.

Step 3: Choose now whether you would like to cut out a "peek hole" inside of the bezel area. This is optional, a matter of personal preference. If you choose to cut out the area behind the stone, it does make the pendant a little lighter and saves some metal clay, which is always good in my book. It is up to you. If you choose to, cut out the hole evenly and consistently around the inside of the bezel wire, rounding out corners. Corners can cause weak areas. It is best not to cut closer than 4 mm to the inside edge of the bezel. There needs to be enough metal clay to hold strong and firm during firing. Let the whole piece dry completely. This will give you a strong foundation on which to work.

Creating the Add-on Templates

Step 1: Make a solid decision about how you will make the bail and where to put it. The bail is an important part of the pendant along with other parts that you will add on. Many times these add-on parts will be an integral part of the bail. The choice was made with this design to place the bail on the back side so it would not interrupt the flow of the composition on the front. There will be another add-on part at the bottom of the pendant.

Step 2: Make a quick sketch of what you have decided to do with the bail and any other elements you have within your design. The sketch does not need to be extensive, just enough to finalize your ideas. These things need to be thought through before you roll out your metal clay. If you put in some time now on planning and construction, then later things will more easily fall into place. Time to work is limited as the metal clay threatens to dry out. Even simple plans are better than no plans at all. For our sample piece, I made a very quick sketch to plan out the bail and other elements to the design.

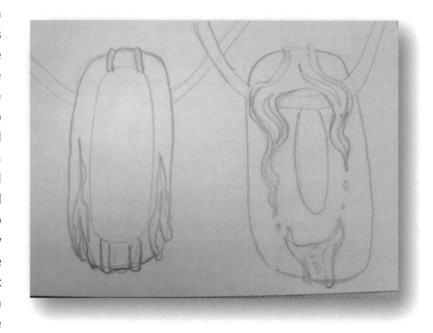

Step 3: Make a template of the piece that will become the bail. Also, make a template for any other added on shape(s). Do this the same way you made a template for the back plate. Lay another sheet of blank paper on top of your sketch and trace the shapes. Cut these pieces out and there you have it. This pendant had two pieces to add on; the bail which wrapped around the top front to the back side and the bottom piece, which also wrapped around from the front to the back. Here are the three templates that were made to create this pendant.

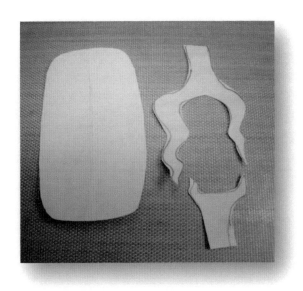

Step 4: Just like a dress may look great on the hanger but may or may not when it is on, trying on the bail template makes it easier to know if the fit is right. To do this, place a straw the size you want your bail to be on the back and mold the paper template around it. Check the fit. Make any modifications to the template if there is a need. Trying on your bail template helps to ensure it fits well and does just what you want it to do. You can be confident to use this template now.

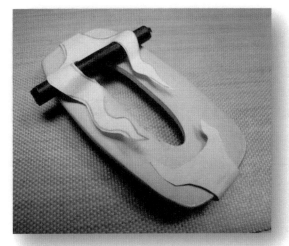

Add on the Bail and Other Elements

Step 1: Sand the back plate. It is important that you have a clean foundation onto which you will be adding all your wonderful design elements. Take the time to file all unwanted lumps and bumps, sand and refine all surfaces so they literally feel as smooth as silk. Start with coarser sanding blocks and work up to finer. All the time you put into creating a beautifully refined foundation will pay off with less work later and you will end up with a strong, beautiful bezel setting without any tears, rips or cracks.

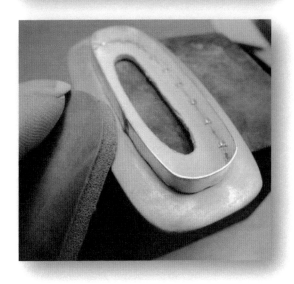

Step 2: Using the remainder of your metal clay, roll out a piece three cards thick. Place your bail template on the metal clay and cut out the shape by tracing the edge of the template with a needle tool. Take away the metal clay surrounding the bail cut-out and put away. With your water sprayer, spritz the bail metal clay lightly with water. The metal clay bail needs to be pliant to bend and mold easily without forming any cracks while being put into place. The water will keep the clay pliant and cooperative.

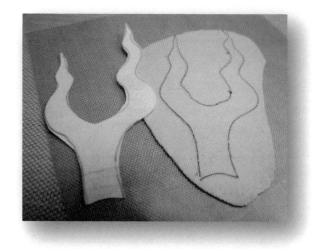

Step 3: Wet the area on the back plate where you will be adding on the pieces with paste. Let the water soak in a moment. Place a straw the size of the bail you'd like on the spot where the bail will be. Put the metal clay bail that you have cut out over the straw and push the metal clay into place with a wet, round brush. Smooth the surface with the brush and use lots of paste to make sure the pieces are attached well. Let this piece dry.

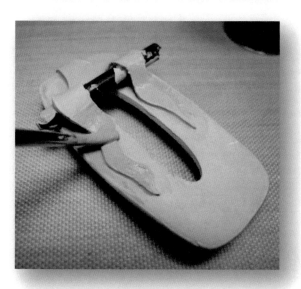

Step 4: Attach any other pieces in the same manner, and then let them dry completely. Once dry, sand and file all surfaces smooth. The goal is to make everything feel as smooth as silk.

Now that all the pieces are attached and refined, the construction phase for this design is complete.

Embellishment

Step 1: Prepare the back plate for embellishment with syringe metal clay. To do this, place your dried piece next to your sketch of the design so it is easier to see. Get a sharp pencil and draw the design directly on the surface of the dry metal clay. These are the lines that will be followed when adding the syringe clay. Doing this takes a lot of the guess work out of the placement of the syringe.

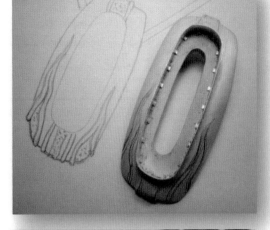

Step 2: Use a small round brush to wet the area where the metal clay syringe will be applied. Let the moisture soak in a few moments so the syringe will adhere easily to the surface of the back plate.

Step 3: Using the syringe metal clay, follow the lines that you have drawn and place the metal clay right where you want it to be. Helpful hint: To prevent messing up the wet syringe that you have so carefully placed in your design, do a quadrant at a time, place it in a dehydrator and let it dry for five minutes, then go on to the next section. Then you don't have to worry about messing up the previous work.

Continue with the syringe metal clay until you have your design complete. The textured areas in this piece were done simply by drawing the outline of the "flames", letting it dry, then filling the area inside the lines with syringe and poking it with a small, round brush to get the rough surface.

The last thing to be done with the syringe is to place a heavy line at the base of the bezel wire. Where-ever the design has not covered the base of the bezel wire it needs to have this line of syringe added to strengthen the bond of the fine silver wire to the metal clay. This also adds a finished look to the bezel at the base.

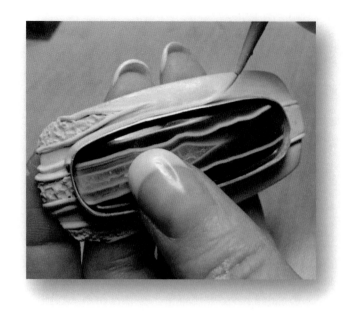

R & R : Refine and Reinforce

Once you have finished placing the syringe and putting all the details into place, let it dry completely. You are now ready for some R & R: refining and reinforcing. This is the time you take for making everything well refined, smooth and ready for the kiln. This is done by filing, sanding and burnishing all surfaces. It needs to feel like silk in your hand. Check all parts that were added on to make sure they are completely reinforced with layers of paste and syringe. The more attention you give to the details here the more it will pay off later with a well-made, solid piece. Sand everything smooth, and I mean everything: front and back, sides and the inside of the bail. Fill in any areas where tiny bubbles may have popped up and sand again. You can't do too much of this—reinforce and refine your piece. It is worth your time and effort.

Using a Casting Investment Chapter 4

To ensure the bezel shape stays in place without any distortion, ceramic fiber paper and a casting investment can be used. Casting investment is a product that is used in casting metals, for making ring pellet castings, or, as in our case, to make placeholders for bezel set stones. The kind of investment used for this demonstration was Cool Tools Ultra Smooth Investment. It dries quickly, within about 30 minutes after pouring into place and will not shrink as it is fired. It pops out easily and leaves the bezel wire in place. With this shape stone, the long, straight sides would very likely be pushed inward under the pressure of firing so an investment was placed inside the bezel area to prevent this.

Step 1: Ceramic fiber paper is a heat-resistant light weight ceramic-impregnated paper that we will use to provide a cover for the opening which was cut out on the back plate of this piece. It will easily pop out after firing, along with the investment. The investment will be poured on top of it, dried and fired together.

Step 2: Place your stone on a single sheet of fiber paper and trace the shape. Cut this out and place it inside the bezel area of your piece. The paper does not have to be perfectly fitted to the sides but it is best if it lies flat within this area. You can see that there are some gaps between the bezel wire and the fiber paper in the picture to the right. This is fine. It will not affect the investment so just cut it out as closely as you can.

Step 3: Place about three tablespoons of investment into a bowl. Add water and stir until the consistency of the investment is like yogurt. If the consistency is too thin, add a little more of the investment and stir until smooth.

Step 4: Place your piece on a flat surface and make sure it is level. This piece has a hidden bail on the back so a pencil was placed under the end, lifting the lower side up to make the bezel area level. Once your piece is level, pour the investment into the bezel wire area up to the top edge. Let this air dry about 30 minutes.

The final preparation for the kiln is burnishing your piece. An agate burnisher does a fine job with this. Rub all areas that you want to be shiny with the side of the agate burnisher. This burnishing will bring out the shine even before it is fired and makes finishing later on easier, after it is fired.

This piece is now ready for firing.

How Firing Effects Your Design

Before you start designing your setting, there are a few things that need to be considered. During the firing process, the organic binders of the metal clay are burned away and the resulting silver particles "sinter," becoming denser and stronger. The burning away of the binders and sintering of the metal causes the piece to shrink in size 8 to 10% in Art Clay silver while retaining its original form. Once completely fired, the remaining piece is composed of 99.9% pure silver. This process does what I call "the big squeeze" and it has multiple effects on your design. Let's take a look at this and what we can do to manage these effects.

I-- Doming effect of the metal clay back plate surrounding the bezel wire.

There is a pulling in or a horizontal movement inward of the shrinking metal clay as it fires. This movement of the back plate hits the vertical wall of the bezel wire. I liken this to an unstoppable force meets an immovable object. This causes the metal clay to push upward as the bezel holds back some of the horizontal force. Since the movement of the metal clay cannot move horizontally as easily when an embedded bezel wire is in place, it will continue pulling in and upward, thus causing the dome.

What to do about it—nothing, not a darn thing. It is going to happen; it is just the nature of the beast so relax about it. I actually like the doming effect and I do not fight it. I go a step further and take advantage of it in many of the designs I place on the back side of my pendants so really, this is nothing to worry about.

2--Doming effect of the metal clay on the inside of the bezel wire area.

The same pulling in of the metal clay while firing may cause a rise in the edges of the cut out area inside the bezel where you will set your stone. This may cause your stone to rock back and forth on the raised edges and not sit straight in the bezel after firing.

What to do about it—after firing, you can gently tap the inside area down with a hammer and dapping tool until it brings the edges that have raised up within the bezel area down and allows the stone to lie flat again.   You can also file down the offending areas until your stone is stable.

3—Cracking or Tearing

Tearing and cracking happen as a result of weak areas giving way to the pressure of the sintering metal.   Cracks follow the path of least resistance, just like a fault line. It is wise to keep this in mind when designing your piece.

What to do about it—before firing, check your work for weak spots. An area that is vulnerable for tearing is the "peek hole" inside the bezel area. If you have cut out this area, make sure it is evenly cut, following the bezel wire without any places that are thinner than others. Another area that can be vulnerable is where the two ends of a band of texture meet like in the picture to the right. Let's take a look at how to fix this situation.

So you've got a crack, let's fix it.

Step 1: Fill the crack with Art Clay Oil Paste using a needle tool. Place a few drops of oil paste directly in the afflicted area. Let it dry completely, 30 minutes at 210F/100C or for 24 hours at room temperature.

Place another layer on top of the first layer if needed. You want to over fill the area so you can file the surface and hide the crack. Let this dry.

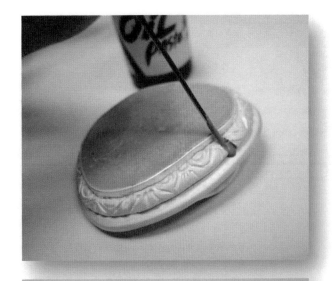

Step 2: Before firing, when the oil paste has been dried, file the oil paste carefully with a small jeweler's file to blend it in with the pattern of the metal clay surrounding it. This will make it easier to conceal the fix later after firing.

Step 3: Fire the piece again at 1472 degrees for thirty minutes. After firing, file and sand the area to blend it in. I do what I call "creative filing" to camouflage the filled in area. The lines in the texture were continued in the mended area by using a small jeweler's file to conceal the fix. Patina and finish the piece as usual. The oil paste does an excellent job of filling in and fusing metal clay and fine silver together. No one would ever know there was a crack the size of the Grand Canyon in this piece. That is one of the wonderful things about metal clay; you can always fix a crack or tear.

4—Distortion of the Bezel Wire Shape

This is the #1 complaint I hear "My stone won't fit in the bezel after firing." Here is what I have observed happens: the pressure of the "big squeeze" during firing can have different effects on different shaped bezels. If you have an oval or round shaped bezel, it will be inherently stronger and hold up better than other shapes. Here is an analogy of how I like to think of the bezel wire:

Think of an arched bridge extending over a deep canyon. Along comes a rumbling, fully laden 18 wheeler to go across this bridge. What happens to the arches under the bridge as the truck passes? They compress and hold as the weight of the truck pushes down on them. The truck goes on its way across to the other side of the canyon. The strength of an arch comes from its shape. When a load is placed on top of an arch, its force spreads out and down the sides of the arch. Now think of a long expanse of a flat bridge. Here comes that same rumbling truck. The weight and pressure push down as before and what do you think happens? The bridge bows at best, giving way to the extra weight. At worst, it breaks as the truck goes plummeting to the canyon below. The breakage is comparable to the snapping of the fused ends of the bezel and it is my hopes of creating a beautiful pendant that go plummeting.

Here is an example of what can happen to the bezel wire under pressure during firing when there is a flat, unsupported area. The top flat part has bowed under the pressure of the shrinking metal clay while the arched bottom part has held up nicely and still fits the stone.

How can this distortion be prevented?

There are a few things that can be done to prevent distortion during firing. Using tabbed, fine silver bezel wire can help. This type of bezel wire has small tabs that are bent both vertically and horizontally on the base of the wire. These tabs act like teeth that grab the metal clay and hold nicely when embedded.

Secondly, while molding the shape of the tabbed bezel wire to fit the stone, make it about 1 mm bigger on all sides of your cabochon. The shape should conform to the stone but still have a bit of room on all sides. The stone should sit on the horizontal tabs of the wire and not fall through when held.

Thirdly, with bezels that have a flat side or sides that can more easily give in to pressure of shrinkage during firing, use casting investment within the bezel area. This substance holds the bezel wire in place during firing as described on page 29. This is a fast and easy way to ensure the shape of the bezel wire will not change due to pressure of the shrinking metal clay.

What was done to correct the situation here was to simply push the bezel wire outward with my thumb until there was enough room to wedge the stone in. The stone could not sit flat on the back plate but there was enough bezel wire to grab the stone and hold it in place when set. This is not ideal, but the end result is better than not being able to set the stone at all. The best thing to do to prevent this situation is to use casting investment to hold the bezel while firing.

Firing Metal Clay

When metal clay is fired, the binders and water content are burned away and the particles of silver are able to fuse together. This process is called sintering. Metal clay particles are uneven and of various sizes, therefore they do not fit together in an orderly way. They fuse as they touch, leaving tiny open spaces of air. Think of a bowl of jelly beans, the uneven beans touch but leave air where their shapes prevent contact. It is the same with metal clay. This is the natural structural form of metal clay.

Supporting Metal Clay During Firing

Flat metal clay pieces can be fired on a kiln shelf, soldering brick or laid on fiber paper. Pieces that have three dimensional forms are best supported in vermiculite, alumina hydrate powder or wrapped in fiber blanket. Please follow manufacturer's safety standards when using these products. Fiber blanket is particularly effective for firing round objects because you can mold the fiber blanket around the piece to support it during firing.

Steps for Firing

Step 1: Place your completely dried metal clay piece in the center of a kiln shelf, supported by any one of the products just mentioned, if needed.

Step 2: Place the kiln shelf on four short posts that raise it up off the bottom of the kiln. This will help the heating to be more even and also make it easier to pick up the shelf and remove your piece when the firing process is complete.

Step 3: Turn on the kiln and set it for the proper temperature, hold time and ramping speed for your type of metal clay. Here is a quick reference chart:

Metal Clay Firing Chart	Temp.	Time
Art Clay 650	1200	30 min.
Regular, Slow Dry, Overlay	1435	5 min.
Art Clay Standard	1472	30 min.
Art Clay Oil Paste	1472	30 min.
PMC Standard	1650	2 hours
PMC +	1470	30 min.
PMC3	1110	30 min.

You're Fired!

Fire your piece at the appropriate temperature, hold time and ramp speed for your type of metal clay. For Art Clay 650 silver, this piece was fired at 1200 degrees (650 C) for 30 minutes at full ramp.

The piece can cool down naturally in the kiln before being taken out or quenched with water. As the piece comes out of the kiln it will have a white, mat surface and the investment will turn brownish yellow.

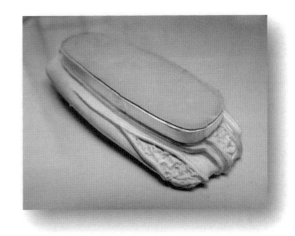

Pop the investments out of the piece by pushing from the back with you thumb. If you have not cut out a "peek hole" in the back, use water to dissolve the fired investment. An old toothbrush works really well to get all of it out.

Use a brass brush to clean up the surface and bring out the silvery color of the metal. Place a dab of dish washing soap on the piece and get the surface wet. Scrub the surface until nearly all the white is gone and the silver color emerges.

Patina: Liver of Sulfur

At times you may want to add a patina to the surface of the setting. This gives your piece an "aged" look, bringing out the texture and adding depth to your composition. Liver of Sulfur (LOS), potassium sulfide, is an oxidation agent used to place a patina on the surface of fired metal clay. It comes in two forms, a solid form and a liquid form. The solid form is mixed with water and diluted. The liquid form can also be diluted in water or painted directly on to the fired metal clay.

> Liver of Sulfur is 'like a box of chocolates; you never know what you're going to get.'

There are many colors Liver of Sulfur can produce, from greens and blues to golds and browns and surprising magentas can develop. However, the rainbow effect and iridescent blending of these colors are somewhat of a difficult thing to predict. As soon as the metal touches the solution, the reaction starts and the surprise of what you will get begins. I always tell my students that Liver of Sulfur is "like a box of chocolates; you never know what you're going to get." Along with the surprising colors is the surprising odor that will hit you as you mix it. My son calls it "the bowl of death" every time I make a batch. The smell of rotten eggs comes to mind. Now, please don't let that intimidate you from ever using it; there are things you can do that help you achieve your desired effect and the smell is quite temporary. Using Liver of Sulfur really is fun and very effective. It definitely adds a bit of adventure to the jewelry making process.

Basic recipe for using Liver of Sulfur:

For lump Liver of Sulfur:

1 lump about a pea size of LOS

1 cup of hot, not boiling distilled water

1 cup of cold water

1 teaspoon of Baking Soda

2 plastic or glass bowls

For Gel Liver of Sulfur:

Dip a paint brush in and whatever clings to it is enough.

1 cup of hot, not boiling distilled water

1 cup of cold water

1 teaspoon of Baking Soda

2 plastic or glass bowls

Heat the cup of distilled water in a small bowl so that it is steaming but not to the boiling point.

Heat will speed up the development of color. Place your LOS in the hot water and stir to dissolve. The water will change to a yellowish color. Both types of LOS work the same but the gel form does not degrade in light and air the way the lump form can during storage. I find the gel form more convenient to use and is a reliable, good product. In the second bowl, pour a cup of cold water and add the baking soda and stir until it is dissolved. Baking soda neutralizes and stops the development of the patina right where it is.

Dip your clean, fired piece of metal clay into the very warm solution. Take it out right away and see what colors you are getting. Dip again until you get the color that you are happy with. Now dip the piece in the cold water and baking soda solution. This will halt the action in its tracks and neutralize the LOS. Dry it off with a paper towel.

The photo on the right shows the piece dipped several times to achieve this very dark color. High contrast was desired for the look of the piece so a black patina was achieved.

Buff the surface with a silver buffing cloth. This will take off the dark patina on all the raised surfaces. The more you buff the lighter the silver will become as the patina is removed. Within the cracks and crevasses the dark patina will stay. This gives an aged look and adds more depth to the textured surface of your metal clay piece.

40

Setting the Stone   Chapter 6

The Art of Persuading the Bezel

In this method of designing from the stone, bezel setting consists of three techniques:

- Embedding the bezel and firing in place
- Fitting the bezel to the stone
- Setting the stone

We have completed the first part of embedding the bezel and it is has been fired. The next technique we will explore is fitting the bezel to the stone.

Every stone is cut differently; the shapes vary and the slope of the sides can be inconsistent, even within the same stone. One side may be higher than another side. In order for the bezel to fit the stone, a bit of customizing is necessary. This will ensure the best setting possible.

Create a Custom Fit

Step 1: Place your stone in the bezel and push it firmly down so that it sits flat in the setting. Observe the profile of the stone next to the bezel. The height of the bezel should be just past the "shoulder" of the stone. The taller the bezel the more material there is to mold to the stone. This can present problems such as buckles or ripples that can form in the bezel. We are trying to avoid this. So a bit of customizing is appropriate.

In the picture to the right the stone slopes down toward the corners, leaving a higher dome of the stone in the middle and a tapering off to thinner edges toward each end. This is quite common and it means that the bezel must be custom fit to hold the stone.

Create a Custom Fit

Step 2: Set your piece on a rubber block to keep it from slipping. Using a flat jeweler's file, file down the sides until they echo the shape of the stone. Begin by filing flat across the bezel to remove material efficiently. Gradually angle the file so with each stroke you will be angling the edge to form a bevel that will lie flat against the stone when set and be easier to burnish as it conforms to the shape of your stone.

Place your stone back inside the bezel and check to see how you are doing. In this picture the right side has a nice slope that echoes the stone. The left side needs a bit more material taken off the bezel to have a consistent fit. The bezel is still too high on the left compared to the right side of the setting. Ideally, you want the bezel to be even all the way around the stone. A little more filing is necessary.

As you are filing the bezel you may find that tiny shards of metal are forming on the inside edge. You'll need to clean up the inside of the bezel. Use a round jeweler's file and rub the inside edge of the newly beveled bezel. This will make all the tiny pieces of metal pop up and are easily removed. If you leave them there they can show up when you are setting the stone, being trapped between the stone and bezel. At that point, they are nasty little guys to clean up, which is what you want to avoid.

Conceal the Joint

Step 3: Using a flat jeweler's file, file down the area where the seam of the two ends of the bezel are fused. The oil paste is easily filed down to the fine silver bezel, concealing where the joint is located. Keep filing to even out the area surrounding the seam. This area will be polished later and you will not see where the two ends meet.

Setting the Stone

When bezel setting a stone, you are capturing the stone in a thin layer of metal. The metal will be molded slowly but firmly around the stone to hold it in the setting. If the process is rushed, buckles or ripples can form. We want to "persuade" the metal to take on a new shape, coaxing it firmly and consistently to transform it from a metal wire into a beautiful bezel that holds the stone gracefully.

Step 1: Place the stone inside the bezel area. Using an agate burnisher, push slightly against the bezel wire inward toward the stone. Make a small indention. It does not have to touch the stone yet. We will get there, but to avoid any unpleasant bumps in the bezel, it is best to do this slowly. For round or oval stones, think of the bezel as a clock face. Using the agate burnisher, to push the bezel gently down over the stone, starting at the 12:00 position. Go to the opposite side, at the 6:00 position and push the bezel wire in slightly. Repeat at the 3:00 and 9:00 positions.

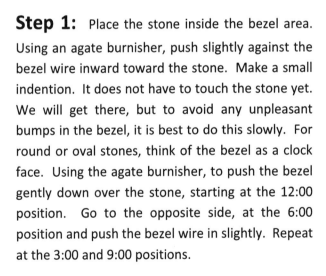

For stones with corners, such as the one here, it is easier to start at a corner first to mold the metal onto the stone. Here I started on the upper left corner, pushing inward slightly. Then go to the opposite lower right corner and push the bezel wire inward, then the upper right corner and the lower left corner respectively. By starting at the corners to set the stone, the bezel will hold the stone in place and you are less likely to create ripples in the metal. Continue working your way around the bezel, always moving back and forth between pairs of opposite positions to distribute the pressure on the stone evenly. Continue patiently until you have pressed the entire bezel evenly around the stone.

Step 2: Using your agate burnisher once again, smooth out the top edge of the bezel. Rub the edge back and forth with the burnisher, creating a smooth, shiny surface. This also rolls the edge up over the stone to make a nice, tight bezel. Be careful not to scrape the stone with the burnisher. Some people tape the top of their stone to help prevent any scrapes or scratches that can happen if your hand slips while pushing the bezel. These scratches that can happen are another reason why I like the more gently "persuasive" method of setting the stone. I am less likely to gouge my stone's surface while pushing the bezel slowly and gently with an agate burnisher.

Finishing

Continue to burnish all areas that are raised in the design. This will produce a bright and shiny contrast to the dark, mat patina. Lastly, give it a good hand buffing.

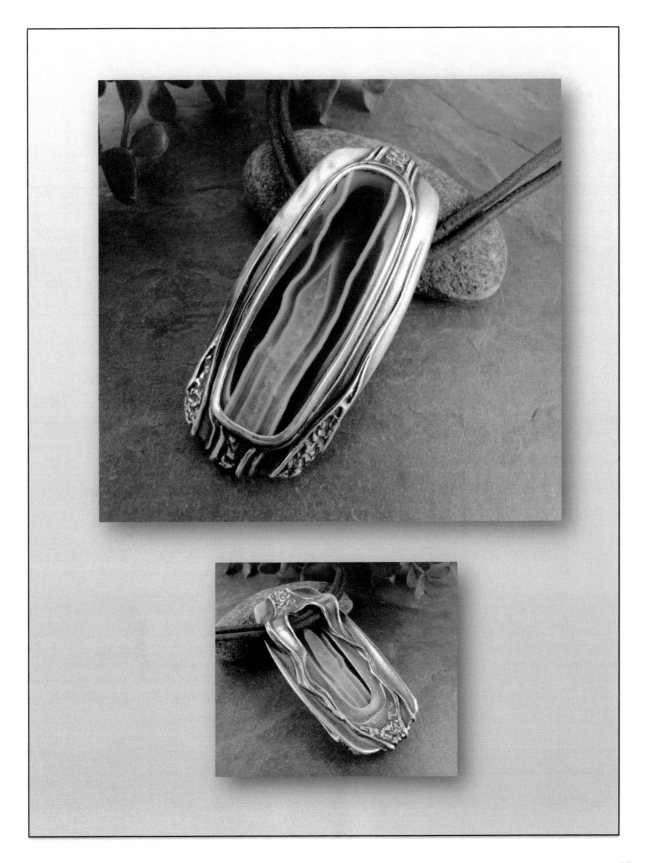

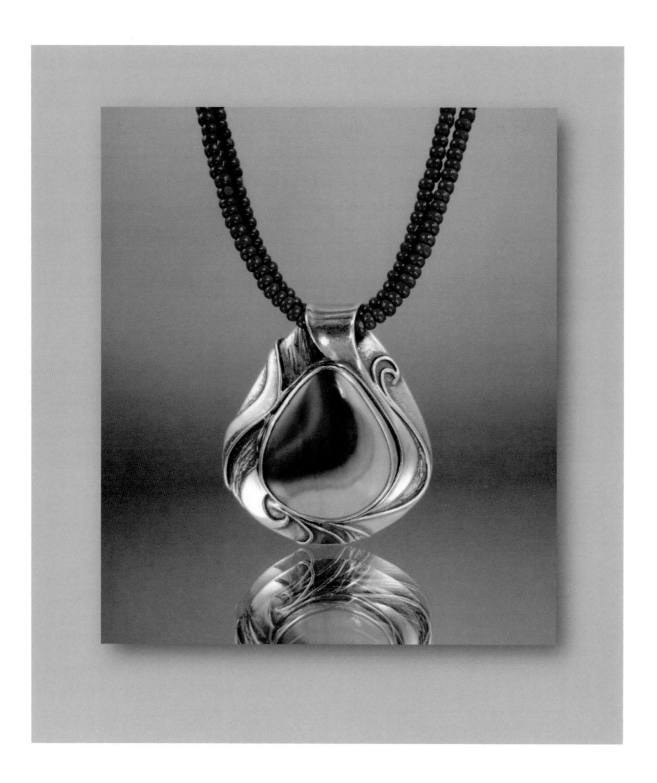

Projects

Chapter 7

Go with the Flow

Imperial Jasper Pendant

Materials: 25 grams metal clay, syringe and paste

Basic Metal Clay Tools

A Great stone

Tabbed Bezel Wire

In the technique of designing from the stone, the main drive of the design is derived from the stone. It is the starting point from which the design emerges so the choice of stone is very important. Here, the flowing lines presented in this Imperial Jasper cabochon were the inspiration for the creation of this setting.

Step 1: Analyze your stone. Refer back to the chart on page 16. What does your stone have to offer in terms of shape, texture and color? What does it not have in terms of those three elements? These things will help you determine what to emphasize in a vivacious stone or what to add to the setting to bring more life to a more subtle stone.

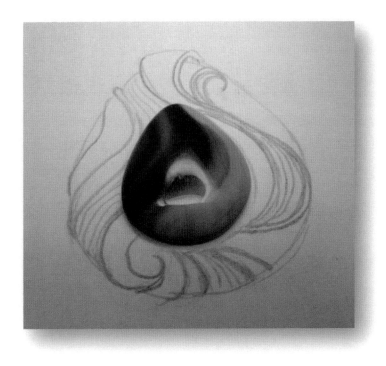

Step 2: Make the sketch of design. Trace the outline of the stone on a blank piece of paper. Now draw the silhouette of the back plate. From here, draw in details of line, form and texture according to what you want to emphasize or add to your stone. The sketch of the design here shows my intent to connect the lines of the setting directly with the flow of line in the stone. The bail was incorporated directly into the design to flow naturally with the lines presented in the stone.

Create the Paper Templates

Step 3: Trace your design on another piece of paper. Cut out the shapes to make templates for your metal clay add-on pieces.

This design had a bail that wrapped from the front to the back so a template was made to fit before the metal clay was opened. Templates for all the add-on pieces were cut out.

Step 4: Wrap the bezel wire loosely around your stone with the tabbed edge toward the back of the stone. Shape the bezel wire so that it conforms to the shape of the stone but fits loosely. Refer to Creating a Bezel Wire on page 20 for more details on how to do this.

Place a few drops of Oil Paste on the seam of the bezel wire. Dry and fire the bezel wire by itself to fuse the ends.

.Prepare the Back Plate

Step 1: Roll out the metal clay to 6 cards thick. Using your paper back plate template, trace the outline with a needle tool. Take the surrounding metal clay and put away in a sealed container.

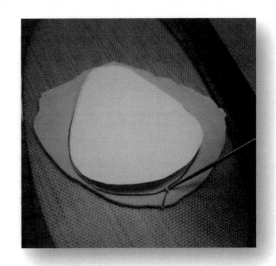

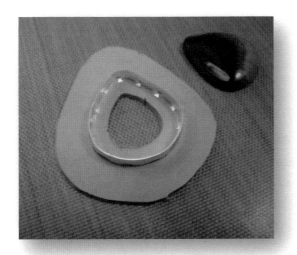

Step 2: Center the fired bezel wire on the surface and push it into the wet metal clay. Push it in just far enough so that the horizontal tabs touch the top of the metal clay.

Cut out the "peek hole" inside the bezel wire, if desired. Make sure you cut an even hole and try not to go any closer than 4 mm to the tabs. This ensures that there will be enough metal clay to support the bezel wire.

Step 3: Let the back plate dry completely.

When dry, file the edges smooth, making sure it conforms to the shape you desire. Sand all surfaces, starting with coarser grit sanding pads, and then moving to finer grit. The back plate should feel as smooth as silk. Remember, this is the base of your project and it is important that you start off with a beautiful foundation. All other pieces are added to this piece so it will behoove you to do it well.

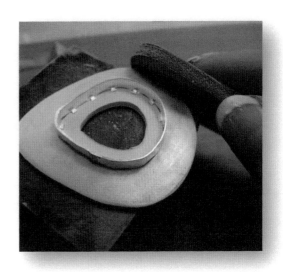

Using the Templates

Step 1: Roll out the remainder of your metal clay three cards thick. Position your bail template on the metal clay and trace the outline with a needle tool.

Remove the surrounding metal clay and put away. Spray the metal clay bail with water so it will remain moist and pliant as you mold it into a bail.

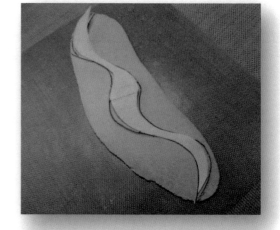

Step 2: Wet the areas that the bail will be attached to with paste. Let this soak in for a moment. Place a straw the size appropriate for the bail on the back plate. Drape the piece of metal clay over the straw, making sure the bail is centered on the back plate and will hold the pendant straight. Smooth out the bail using a wet, round brush.

Let this dry completely before moving on.

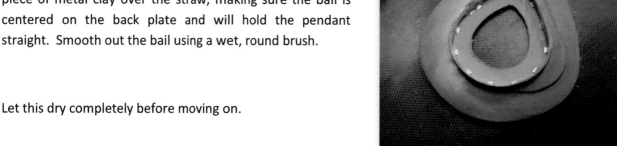

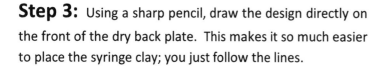

Step 3: Using a sharp pencil, draw the design directly on the front of the dry back plate. This makes it so much easier to place the syringe clay; you just follow the lines.

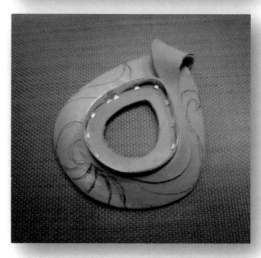

Step 4: Using all other paper templates, cut out the add-on parts. Roll out the metal clay three cards thick; place the templates on top of the clay and cut out the shapes with a needle tool. Wet the areas they will be attached to on the back plate with paste and place them in the appropriate spot, according to the design drawn on the surface.

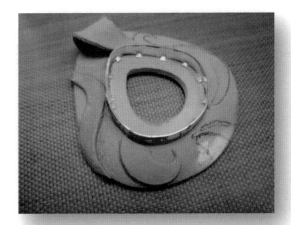

Step 5: Using a small carving tool, carve out lines next to the add-on piece to add a bit of contrast in texture and color. Be careful not to cut too deeply. Keep them light, on the surface and uniform in depth. If you cut more deeply in one area than another, you may be building in a weak spot that may give in to pressure as it is fired. You want to think of uniform strength surrounding your bezel.

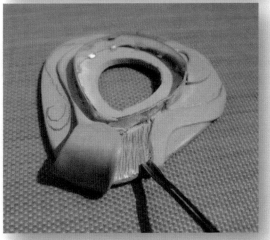

Step 6: Attach all add-on parts to the back side just as you did the front, using paste and a round brush.

Place syringe metal clay and complete your design by following the lines that were drawn on both the front and the back. Also place a heavy line of syringe at the base of the bezel wire. Reinforce the dry syringe with at least two layers of paste.

Fire, Set and Finish

Once the piece has dried thoroughly, take the time to refine all surfaces. When you are satisfied with the how the piece looks and feels; (it needs to feel silky smooth in your hand), place it in the kiln to be fired. Set your kiln for the appropriate temperate and hold time for the type of metal clay you are using. This piece was made with Art Clay 650 slow dry. It was fired at 1200 degrees, held for 30 minutes.

When placing a piece with a hidden bail in the kiln, it is best for it to lay flat. This is hard to do when the bail is sticking out, getting in the way. I don't want the weight of the piece to push on the bail to distort the shape while it is firing and I don't want to flip it over and lay it on the bezel wire either. So, my solution was to dig out different sized holes in one of my kiln shelves. These holes allow the bail to have room while the back plate is lying flat on the shelf. If a pendant doesn't fit in an existing hole, I dig a new one.

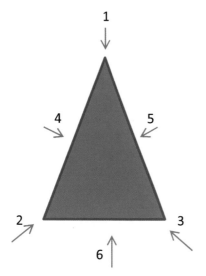

When setting a stone in a triangular shaped bezel, start at the corners, pushing in the points first, locking the stone in the center of the bezel. Slowly mold the corners inward with the burnisher, evenly distributing the pressure of the wire on the stone. The straight sides are carefully pushed inward after the corners; this way you are less likely to bunch up the metal. See the section on Setting Stones on page 41 for more details.

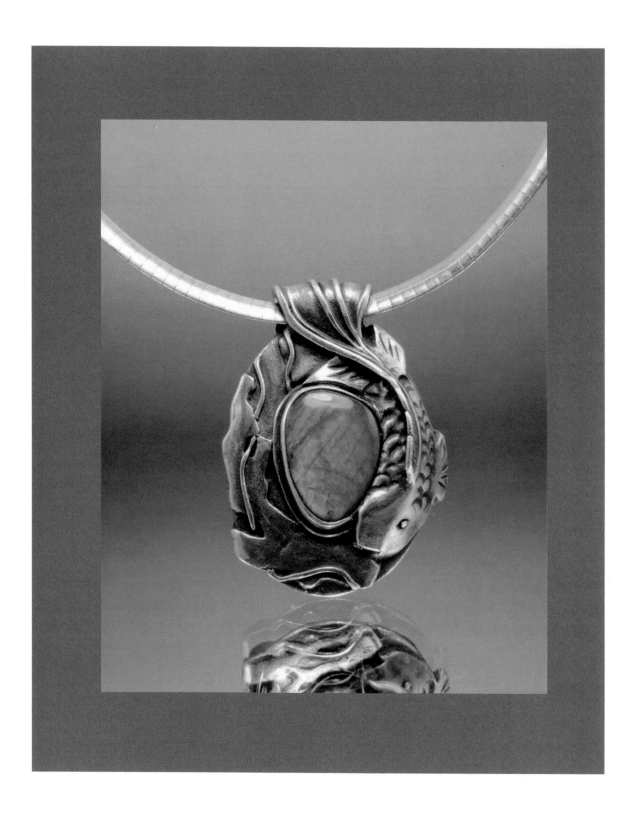

Koi Fish Pendant

Chapter 8

The design of this pendant was inspired by the color of this Labradorite stone. The intense blue/green flash of color brought to mind water and other creatures that live within. This project also shows how to make a more three dimensional setting to add depth to a composition of the pendant.

Materials: 35 grams of Metal Clay syringe and paste

Basic Metal Clay Tools

Tabbed Bezel Wire

A Great stone

Step 1: Trace the outline of the stone on a clean piece of white paper. Draw the silhouette of the back plate. Sketch out the design. It is OK if you don't get it right the first time. It sometimes takes a few tries to zero in on what you are thinking about. This sketch took four tries to figure out the placement of the fish and seaweed. Just keep trying and you'll get there.

The bail was incorporated into the design by elongating the tail of the fish so it would flow over from the front to the back.

Step 2: Trace the sketch onto another piece of paper. Cut out templates of the shapes; one for the back plate and all other pieces to be added on.

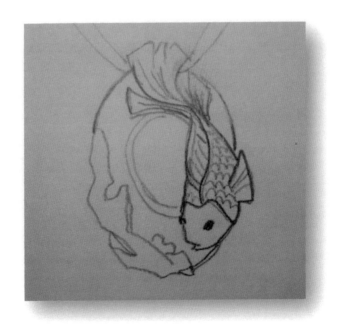

Step 3: Mold the tabbed bezel wire around your stone to get the proper fit, place oil paste on the seam and let it dry completely. Fire the bezel wire by itself and let cool. For details of this process, see Creating the Wire Bezel on page 22.

Step 4: Roll out the metal clay 5 cards thick. Use the back plate template to cut out the metal clay for the design. For more details on this process, see Creating the Back plate, page 23.

Press the fired bezel wire into the center of the metal clay just until the horizontal tabs touch the top of the metal clay. Cut out the center "peek hole," leaving about 4 mm around the inside edge.

Let the back plate completely dry. Sand the surface and all the edges smooth. To strengthen the bezel, a line of syringe clay was placed at the base of the bezel where the wire meets the back plate.

Step 5: Make templates of all add-on pieces. Trace your sketch and cut out the shapes to make templates. Try on your templates to see how they fit. Wrap the paper templates around the back plate as you see here. You may need to make some adjustments. If so, trim the templates to fit the metal clay back plate now before you open your metal clay.

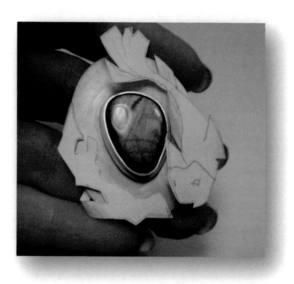

Step 6: In order for the Koi fish to appear more three dimensional, a small amount of metal clay was placed underneath the area where the koi fish cut-out will be on the pendant. This helped round out the body of the fish.

Step 7: Roll out the remaining metal clay two cards thick. Using the paper template of the "seaweed," cut out a portion of metal clay with a needle tool. Take away the surrounding metal clay and put away in an air tight container. Spritz the metal clay with water to keep it moist and maleable. This piece of metal clay is going to be wrapped around the edge of the backplate. Anytime you are going to bend a piece of metal clay it is best to spray it so it is less likely to form cracks as it is put in place.

Step: 8 Wet the area you want to add the "seaweed" to with paste. Let this sit for a minute to soak in. Place the "seaweed" in its spot and use more paste to seal the edges. Smooth the top with a wet round brush. Let this dry before moving on.

When dry, sand and refine the "seaweed" section. It doesn't have to be kiln ready yet, just refined and smooth. We are going to be adding syringe on top of this section and it is easier to smooth out the base before anything is added.

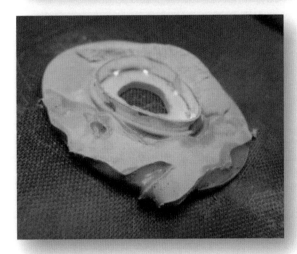

Step 9: Roll out some metal clay three cards thick. Using the fish template, trace the outline using a needle tool and cut out the metal clay. Put the surrounding metal clay away. Spray the cut out lightly with water. Prepare the area to receive the cutout by painting on a generous amount of paste. Let this soak in a minute. Place a straw the size appropriate for the bail at the top of the pendant. Lay the fish cut out in place and wrap the tail over the straw to the back side. Use a wet round brush to mold the cut out into place and smooth the surface. To make the texture for the "scales," the end of a paper clip was used as a tool to make the marks down the side of the fish.

Embellishment

Step 1: Now the fun part of adding all the little details begins! But before you add anything to your emerging masterpiece, you must sand and smooth the base. The fish head was sanded smooth and also the tail. Along the sides, before the fin was added, these areas were cleaned up and made ready. It is worth it to work clean and refine as you go.

Step 2: Roll out a bit more metal clay three cards thick and cut out a thin, long triangle for the dorsal fin. Put it in place with paste and smooth with a wet round brush. Fill all cracks with syringe clay and smooth out with a wet, flat brush. Add the details with syringe on the seaweed, dorsal fin and tail area. Use a small carving tool to carve out the details on the pectoral fins and tail. Have fun with this; there are so many things you can do.

Step 3: Let the piece dry completely. When dry, lightly sand all surfaces, front and back until they feel like silk. The piece needs to look good and feel good.

Prepare for Firing

Mix a small amount of casting investment and pour into the bezel area. For details on this process, refer to the section on Casting Investment on page 29 and 30. Let this dry.

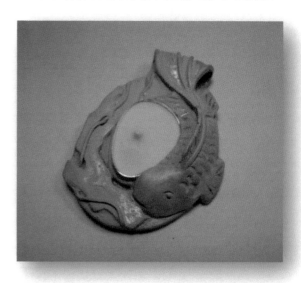

Fire

Once the piece is refined and casting investment has been placed in the bezel area and dried, fire at the appropriate temperature and holding time for your metal clay.

When the piece comes out of the kiln, pop the investment out by pushing from the back until it gives way.

The surface needs to be brushed. Use a brass brush with a dab of dish soap and water. Brush the surface until the silver shines and most of the white is gone.

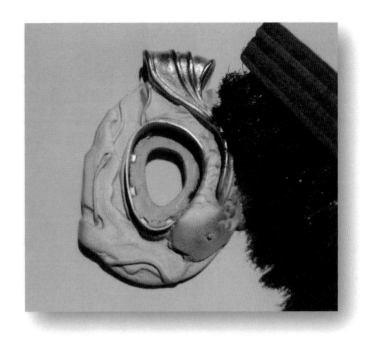

Patina

Add a dark patina to the surface of the fired metal clay. Mix up a small batch of Liver of Sulfur and dip the piece until the desired color is achieved. For detailed instructions on Liver of Sulfur, refer to the section on Patina: Liver of Sulfur, pages 38 and 39.

Setting the Stone

To bezel set a stone in a setting that has a dimensional figure or a heavy design that comes up to the top of the bezel wire presents unique challenges. The Koi fish figure creates a high wall, so to speak, of metal clay leaning up against the bezel wire. During firing, the metal clay will most likely fuse to the fine silver bezel. This will make the bezel in this area nearly impossible to move inward as you would when normally setting the stone.

Since this wall of metal formed in the design will not move, you will need to use it as a solid base to push the stone up against when first starting to set the stone. Start on the opposite side of the wall to do the first push. Start the process by using an agate burnisher, push the bezel inward toward the stone at this spot. If there are corners on your stone, go to them next and begin the process of easing in the bezel. Pressing the corners at the beginning of the process will help prevent the metal from bunching up or forming lumps.

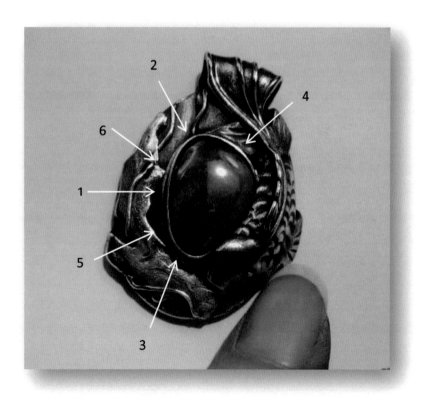

Bezel setting takes practice. Take it slow; try not to get ahead of yourself. Work evenly on opposing sides until the stone is set smoothly.

This picture shows the order of the steps taken to set the stone as the process began. It takes a gentle hand, moving the bezel wire only slightly with each push of the burnisher against the wire. Large movement of the bezel wire makes it easier to cause ripples in the metal that are difficult to smooth out. Refer to the section on Setting the Stone on pages 41 – 44 for more details on this technique.

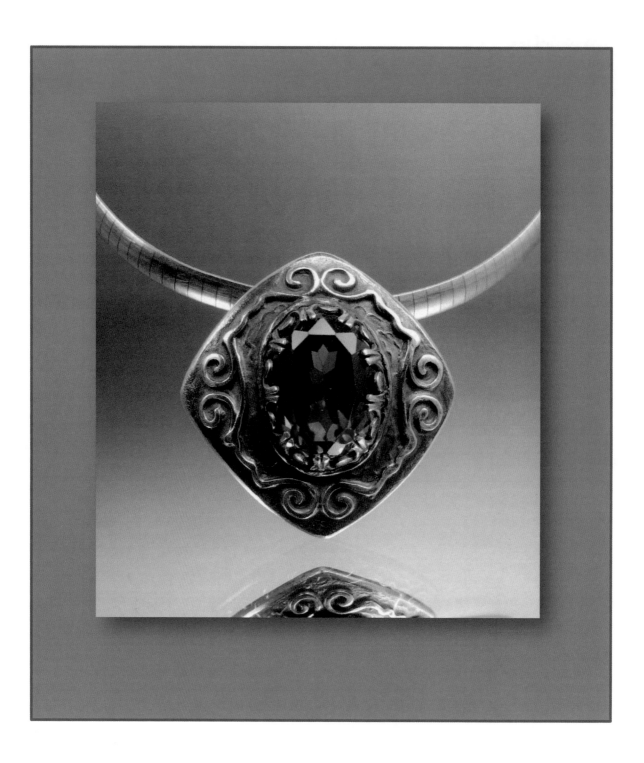

Project

Chapter 9

The Royal Treatment

This project uses sterling silver gallery wire for the bezel. To fuse the two types of metals, fine silver, which is 99.99% pure silver to sterling, which is 92.5% silver and 7.5% copper, you must complete a process called depletion gilding. This is essentially depleting the copper from the surface of the sterling so that it leaves a layer of fine silver on the surface and the two metals are able to fuse more successfully.

Depletion gilding gives you a great deal of freedom to add sterling pieces to your metal clay pieces to add strength or detail.

For this project a sketch was not necessary. I could see the design I wanted by choosing a texture plate with a design that went with the feeling of the stone.

This texture was chosen for its shape and style. The gallery wire has a beautiful, regal feeling that goes with the Alexandrite stone. To get a good visual of this, wrap the wire around the stone and place it on top of texture sheet. Also place the template on top of the texture sheet to define the outer edge of the pendant. Now you can see what the design will look like when complete.

Depletion Gilding

Gallery wire is sterling silver which contains copper and it will not fuse to fine silver. The surface needs to be prepared so that the copper content will not oxidize and prevent a good fusion. A product called Silver Prep was used to do this. Bring 1 cup of water to boil and dissolve 1 tablespoon of Silver Prep in the water. Place the gallery wire in and boil until the surface turns white. This takes about 10 minutes.

Prepare the Gallery Wire

Step 1: Cut the gallery wire to fit your stone. Make the size close to 1 mm bigger around the stone. You want a little wriggle room to make up for the squeezing of the metal clay as it shrinks against the wire. Cut the wire so that it continues the pattern as closely as you can. It is better to go a little bigger to get the pattern right than smaller.

Here in the picture the gallery wire was cut on a slight angle on both sides to match up the pattern.

Here you can see that the gallery wire was cut so it is about 1 mm bigger around the stone.

Step 2: Dab a drop of Oil Paste on the seam of the gallery wire using a needle tool. Let it dry completely. Add one more drop of Oil Paste on the seam and let this dry. This will fill the seam and act as solder to fuse the two ends together.

Step 3: Fire the gallery wire separately at the recommended temperature for Oil Paste, 1472 degrees for 30 minutes at full ramp.

Here is what the gallery wire looks like when it comes out of the kiln. The sterling wire is darkened because of the oxidation of the copper content. The fine silver oil paste is light silver.

Prepare the Back Plate

Step 1: Roll out your clay 6 cards thick. Press this onto the texture plate for the impression of the texture.

Step 2: Now use your template to cut out the shape. I chose a rounded square template that fit the design. Cut the shape with the needle tool.

Step 3: Push the gallery wire into the wet metal clay. Be careful not to push all the way through. Only push it in about half way in. The gallery wire will act as a cookie cutter if you push it in too far. We will be designing the back side and this will reinforce the back and help strengthen and prevent any tearing that may occur from the gallery wire.

Step 4: Cut out a center portion inside the gallery wire. Be careful not to get closer than 4 mm to the gallery wire. There needs to be room for shrinkage. This will allow enough metal clay to strengthen the base where the gallery wire is embedded.

This piece will now be called the back plate. Let it dry completely before working more on it.

Refine the Back Plate

When it has dried, place it on your rubber block. It will not slide as easily when placed on a rubber block. Also, the piece is raised up so you can work more easily. Use one of the coarse sanding pads to start with; sand down the edges so they are nice and smooth. Don't forget to file the inside of the cut out area, too. Use your jewelers file and refine all edges.

Embellishment

Step 1: Prepare the area where you want to place the syringe clay. Use a round brush and wet the area with water and let it soak in a moment.

Step 2: Touch the tip of the syringe down and raise it up while pushing the end so metal clay is being squeezed out. Work above the back plate, letting gravity drop the syringe into place while guiding it with the tip. This takes practice but you'll get it. Touch the tip back down again and stop squeezing to stop the syringe.

Step 3: Place a thick line of syringe at the base of the gallery wire. This will reinforce the bond between the gallery wire and the back plate.

Step 4: Using a small round brush, paint in some paste type or slip around the syringe. This will reinforce the bond and make the syringe look like it is part of the original design, not just sitting on top but integrated into the design. When the paste dries, there may be little bubbles that formed. File those down and add another layer of paste on top. Smooth it all out and let it dry.

The Back Side Design

To begin the back, start with the bail. Roll out the remainder of your clay 3 cards thick. Using the template of graduated sizes, cut out a square the same size as the square you cut for the back plate. Then, use a smaller square in the template, center it and cut that out. You now have a perimeter square that will fit on the back of your piece. We are going to use this as a bail. While you have the clay rolled out, use the end of your drinking straw and cut out three round pieces of clay. Stack the three pieces like a little pile of pancakes. Set the stack aside.

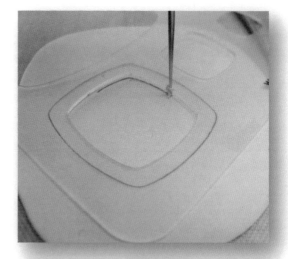

Place the drinking straw at the top corner and lay the square of wet metal clay carefully over the piece and the straw. Make sure the straw is sitting straight so your bail will also be straight. Keep the top surface wet so you can more easily smooth out the clay with your round brush.

Pick up your little stack of metal clay pieces and place them under the square cut out, at the top of the bail.

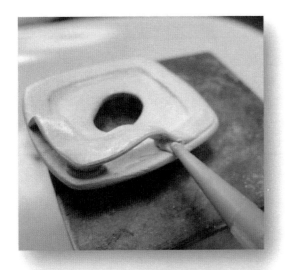

Use your syringe to fill in the area where the two pieces meet the bail. This will reinforce the bail while making it look smooth and seamless.

Do this on both sides and around the little stack.

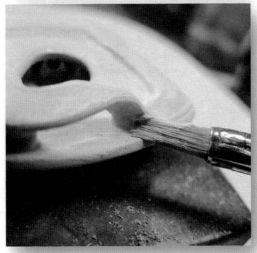

Use a flat brush to smooth out the syringe.

Draw the Design on the Back

Use a sharp pencil to draw your design on the back. Plan where you want to sign the piece and where you want to add some embellishment.

Here I have drawn out where I want to place the syringe, two little balls of clay and a tiny name plate in the middle. This makes it easier to place the syringe.

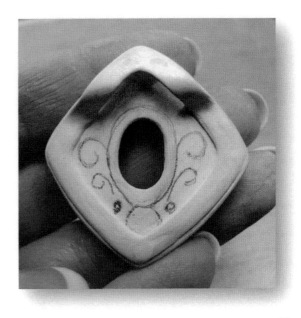

Add Syringe Details

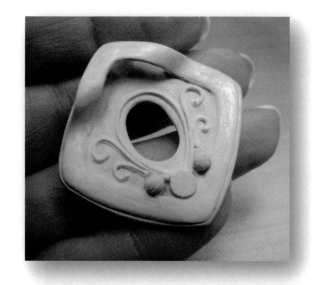

Wet the area you are adding the syringe with water. Let this soak in a bit. Follow the lines that were drawn on the back with the syringe metal clay. A few details were added with the syringe. Have fun with this. The back is an area where you can be a little bit freer to design something more light hearted and playful if you so choose.

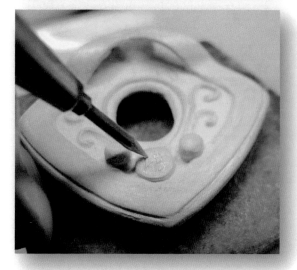

A large needle can be used to etch your initials on the back side if you do not have a scribe like the one I have in this picture.

Make sure everything is smooth and reinforced. Sand every surface so it feels as smooth as silk. Also make sure that the piece is completely dry before putting it in the kiln.

Fire your piece at the manufacturer's suggested settings. For Art Clay 650, 1200 degrees for 30 minutes at full ramp. When it is done firing, it is a white matte finish like in the picture here. Use a brass brush to scrub the surface and bring up the silvery shine. Wet the piece with water and a dab of soap to scrub and burnish the surface. You'll easily see the silver reveal itself as you scrub.

Patina Time

Here is the piece after I have brushed it and before I have placed a patina on the surface. This is completely optional. I do it because I think the darkened crevasses bring out the texture and make the piece look aged, which I love. So I will dip this piece in Liver of Sulfur to darken it. For details on this process, see page 38 and 39.

Also notice here how the metal clay acts as it shrinks around the bezel wire. The back plate will dome slightly, arching toward the back. This is natural as the metal clay shrinks and the gallery wire does not. I actually love the graceful dome. It would take a lot of work to do that manually so I welcome it and work with it to make it what I believe is an asset to metal clay bezel setting.

Here is what the piece looks like right after I have taken it out of the Liver of Sulfur. It is almost black.

Now it is time to polish the front and back. Use a polishing cloth to shine up the highlights. The syringe areas will become very shiny for strong contrast against the texture of the rest of the piece.

Setting the Stone

Setting a stone with gallery wire is such a pleasure. It is much easier than a straight bezel wire even though many things to do are the same. You still want to roll the bezel to the stone in a clock wise motion. Starting at 12:00 and using your agate burnisher, push the prongs of the gallery wire down onto the stone. Now push the prongs at the 6:00 position down onto the stone. Next you'll do the same at the 3:00 position and then the 9:00 position. You are trapping the stone with the wire to hold it to the back plate. Continue pushing all of the sides in evenly so they curve gracefully over the edge of the stone and hold it tightly.

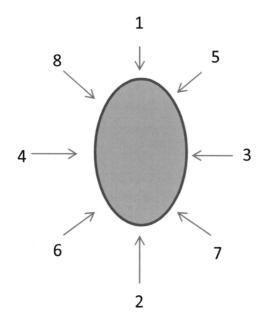

Part 4

Unusual

Settings

Think out of the box...

Rock in the Cradle

A "cradle" of metal clay was designed to hold this unusual stone.

Embedded Wire Setting

Fine silver wire was embedded in the silver metal clay to provide the setting for this Ammonite Fossil. The wire was molded to the lines of the stone to hold the stone in place.

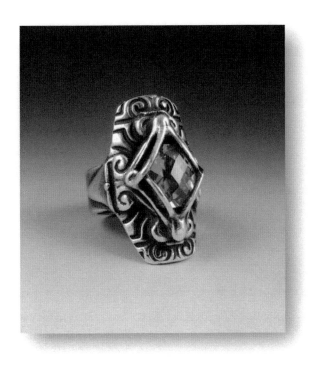

Syringe as the Bezel

The bezel for the stone was made with two bands of syringe metal clay. The stone was fired in place.

Setting the Stone Backwards

Sunset Through the Trees

To create this setting, the inspiration was drawn from the bright coloring in the stone. The intent was to frame what was to be a sunset as if it was being viewed through a forest. The stone was set with the back side of the stone showing through the frame on the front. Wires were embedded in the back to hold the cabochon in place after firing.

The sketch that was drawn helped in visualizing the placement of the trees and getting the right proportion. The tree on the left was meant to look as if it were closer than the three trees on the right.

The template for the back plate was made from this simple drawing.

Four pairs of 20 gauge fine silver wires were embedded in the metal clay on the back side of the pendant. There was a pair of wires for every corner.

Black polymer clay was rolled out to make a coil. The coil was fitted to the stone like a frame. This gave the stone some cushion against the wire and held it in place tightly.

Shrinkage was taken into account when placing the wires. They were spaced with enough room around the edge of the stone so that after firing, there would be enough room for the stone and the polymer clay within the hold of the wires.

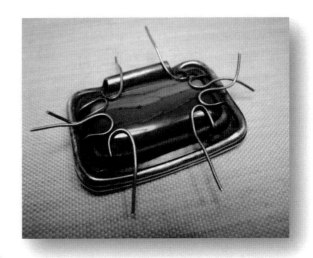

The wires were bound together with half round sterling wire three times at each place they touched. After binding, the wires were trimmed and bent into curls which tightened the hold they had on the stone. I have found that it works better to bind the wire together first and then tighten by curling the ends.

Learning from Sketches and Templates

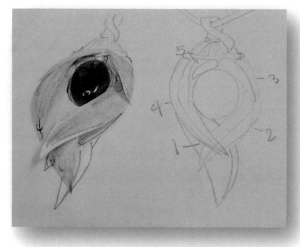

Waiting for Spring

I learned a couple of things while making the templates for this Labradorite piece. First, laying the paper templates on top of each other and seeing the pattern that the metal clay would make was very helpful in the planning phase of this piece. The paper templates helped me plan the order in which I would lay the metal clay leaves down.

The second thing I learned was that literally molding the paper into the shapes of the design was very helpful to see what the clay will do before you cut the clay. The overlapping leaves of the paper templates showed me that I was not going to be physically able to set the stone where the leaves covered the stone. To remedy the situation, I decided to partially set the stone in the area under the leaves before it was fired and before the leaves were added. I had to do this delicately so I did not break the unfired back plate while pushing the bezel. I left enough room for the stone to slide out in the front section. I then completely set the stone after the piece was fired.

Aslan

An important thing I learned making this sculptural piece was that by using multiple layers of the same template, I could create a three dimensional effect of the lion's face. The first template was the outline of the mane, which essentially was the back plate.

The second template of the lion gave the outline of the face and separated the mouth. The third template of the lion's face had the eyes and nose cut out so I could mark the place where these features would be set. I did not have to guess using the templates.

Another thing I learned from Aslan was that the shrinkage of the clay has an effect on the look of the eyes. I was trying really hard to get the eyes to have the look of a lion but as they fired, the eyes got bigger and more round, making them look more human. The shrinkage of the metal clay pulled the metal back, opening his eyes more than I anticipated. He went from having smaller, more lion eyes before firing to larger, more human looking eyes after firing. So now I know to make the eyes a bit smaller, knowing they will widen in the firing process.

About the Author

Lisa Barth is a Senior level certified Art Clay instructor from Atlanta, Georgia. She teaches from her home studio and travels the country to bring her unique techniques of design and bezel setting to others. Lisa is also teaching jewelry photography and has had her photos published in several magazines. Her metal clay work has been published in Metal Clay Artist Magazine and an article written on the same subject. Lisa was chosen to be a contributing artist to Holly Gages' calendar; The Art and Design of Metal Clay Jewelry 2011

In addition to metal clay, Lisa is a wire jewelry artist and actively teaches and loves sharing her passion for this art. She has been published in several magazines, including the cover of Bead&Button, Australian Beading, BeadStyle, Metal Clay Artist Magazine, and Bead&Button's Creative Beading Vol. 4. Her work has been featured in Barbara McGuire's book *Creative Canes* and she has appeared on Live television, presenting her work.

Bezel setting stones is her specialty and Lisa enjoys sharing her expertise in designing organically, achieving harmony between stone and setting. She is always learning and pushing herself to achieve excellence.

"I haven't made it yet but I intend on taking a lifetime to get there. Anyone wishing to learn with me can come on aboard. Life is short, let's have some fun!"

Ammonite Wonder

Natural fossil cabochon set in metal clay.

Bibliography

Aimone, Steven. *Expressive Drawing.*

New York: Lark Books, 2009.

Leland, Nita. *The New Creative Artist.*

Cincinnati, Ohio: North Light Books, 2006.

Bayles, David, and Ted Orland. *Art & Fear.*

Santa Cruz, CA: The Image Continuum, 1993.

Wikipedia, Color Star. 2007

Product Sources

Dale Penrod—great cabs!

www.designer-cabs.com

Tools:

www.CoolTools.com

www.ArtClayWorldUSA.com

www.naturescapesstudio.com

www.artclaysociety.com

www.metalclayfindings.com

www.jffjewelersupply.com

12551190R00055

Made in the USA
Lexington, KY
15 December 2011